The Prestige

Midland General

Notts & Derby/Mansfield District

John Banks
Photography by G H F Atkins

Cover: In a rare prewar colour view, Midland General AEC Regent/Weymann No. **50 (DNU 968)** shares the limelight with East Midland Eastern Coach Works-bodied Leyland Tiger TS7 No. **E79 (CRR 679)**.

Rear cover: Before the advent of the National Bus Company and its bland corporate liveries, Midland General's blue and cream livery stood out among those of other Tilling fleets in red or green. This was particularly evident on the Bristol RELH6G coaches of 1964. Number **31 (1385 R)** was at Broad Marsh bus station, Nottingham, in October 1964.

Title page: In an early postwar scene at Nottingham's King Street/Queen Street trolleybus terminus, a snow-encrusted Notts & Derby vehicle has just arrived after struggling through from Ripley.

Opposite page: Midland General 1948 AEC Regent Mark III No. **86 (MRB 31)** waits at Mount Street bus station, Nottingham, in January 1950 before departing for Ripley on the NDT A4 service: MGO provided vehicles on hire to NDT.

Below: The Bristol Lodekka became the group standard double-decker. Three late FLF6Gs in the Midland General fleet, **SRB 71/3/6F**, stand at Mount Street in May 1968.

Pages 4/5: The four faces of the group's double-deck fleet: pre- and postwar AEC Regents, the Bristol KSW and the Bristol Lodekka.

Introduction

The standardisation of many bus operators' fleets in the postwar period was in some ways an integral part of their fascination; London Transport and the Tilling fleets were the best examples of that. There was something comforting in the knowledge that some high standards were being maintained and that there were unlikely to be any surprises round the corner. And yet...

There was at the same time a dichotomous wish that London had not so ruthlessly done away with its wonderful liveries of prewar origin or that the Tilling group had not pinned its flag so firmly to the Bristol/Eastern Coach Works mast; or that - having done so - it should have not painted everything red or green. There *were* one or two surprises round the corner, in fact, as when Bristol KSWs and Lodekkas in the former Balfour Beatty Nottinghamshire fleets were encountered in a fine, traditional, deep blue and cream livery. Non-standard liveries were encountered by enthusiasts in Scotland, too, and there is a Scottish connection with the Balfour Beatty blue and cream in that it was brought, around 1930, by an incoming General Manager, Mr Hayes, from Scottish General, with whom he had served in a similar capacity.

The Balfour Beatty group was perhaps more important as a member of the electricity supply industry than as an operator of public transport. Thus, when the electricity industry was nationalised by the Labour government in 1948, Balfour Beatty's transport interests were included and were the only passenger transport undertakings that can be accurately described as having been nationalised. Other companies, the Tilling empire being the biggest, became state-owned through voluntary sale. An interesting point about the Balfour Beatty nationalisation is that Midland General, Notts & Derby and Mansfield District were administered for a short time by the British Electricity Authority.

The three above-named operators are the subject of this book. All operated in, or near to, the east-midland city of Nottingham, and thus they had the good fortune to be recorded on film by Geoffrey Atkins, who was born in that city in 1912 and still lives there as these words are being written in early 2003.

The Mansfield District Traction Company (dating

The tramway era - not destined to last beyond the early 1930s for the Group - is represented in these views of the terminus at Ripley with Notts & Derby No. 24, a United Electric covered-top car; and a Mansfield District Hurst Nelson car at Mansfield depot. (Photographers unknown)

*The "trolleybus in the landscape" in Nottingham was more often than not a green Nottingham City Transport vehicle - frequently a six-wheeler, a type not represented in the Notts & Derby fleet. When a Notts & Derby four-wheeler came along, it was immediately identifiable from its blue livery. Here a Weymann-bodied BUT 9611T, No. **343 (NNU 224)**, passes Basford Gasworks at Valley Road, Nottingham, in December 1952. The vehicle had been in service since 1949.*

under this title from 1929) was the oldest of these three companies, having been founded in 1901 as the Mansfield and District Light Railway Company. In 1906 the latter became a subsidiary of Mansfield and District Tramways Ltd and there were further changes, including altering the name in 1933 to Mansfield District Omnibus Company Ltd, before the title Mansfield District Traction Company reappeared as the result of a reconstruction of interests in 1937.

Twelve open-top cars had been run from 1905 on just over twelve miles of track. The fleet had more than doubled by the time trams were abandoned in 1932. The replacement motorbus routes were operated inititial with a fleet of 34 AEC Regents. Unlike a number of the operators that have featured in earlier *Prestige Series* volumes, Mansfield District did not take over many competitors, such activity being confined to a dozen or so operators, none of them very big. The Ebor Bus Company Ltd and Bevan & Barker, both of Mansfield, were purchased in the 1950s.

In 1972 the Company's management was merged with that of East Midland.

The Nottinghamshire and Derbyshire Traction Company, also a tramway operator, dated from 1903. Control (as did that of Mansfield and District) passed to the Tramways, Light and Power Company Ltd in 1913, which was owned by Balfour Beatty & Co Ltd. In 1922 the Midland Counties Electric Supply Company took over from the T L & P Co Ltd. Notts & Derby, as it was universally known, ran trams on 15 miles of track, of which just under four were either leased or used under running rights from Nottingham Corporation. A logical junction with the tracks of Mansfield District was never made, although powers existed for the necessary trackwork to be laid. The complete route - not opened in full until January 1914 - ran from Ripley into the centre of Nottingham: at over 15 miles the second longest tram route in the country - second only to Glasgow Corporation. Twenty-four cars made up the fleet: twelve each open- and covered-top.

The 3ft 6ins-gauge Ilkeston system was purchased in 1913 and run until 1931, with Notts & Derby's own system being abandoned in 1932/3. Trolleybuses replaced both systems, which were connected between Heanor and

Ilkeston, and ran until abandonment in 1953, when the entire fleet was sold to Bradford Corporation, which, under the pro-trolleybus management of Chaceley Humpidge, was seeking an economic method of retaining electric traction and continued to run trolleybuses until 1972 - the last such system in Britain.

Notts & Derby as a motorbus operator became, following the postwar nationalisation, one of the more interesting Tilling fleets by virtue of its magnificent deep-blue and cream livery. At the end of 1971 all its routes were transferred to Midland General, pending an administrative reorganisation.

The Midland General Omnibus Company Ltd was somewhat younger, having begun motorbus operations in 1922, though in existence since 1920. The Company was soon to become the biggest of the three, largely through acquisitions of competing operators, expansion in the first half of the 1930s being particularly noteworthy. In its early years, the Company's Chairman, Sir Joseph Nall, DSO, MP, held the same position with the other two companies.

Although many companies were extremely image-conscious in the prewar period and were not slow in the matter of fleet renewal, Midland General was remarkable in the years from 1936 for the speed with which it modernised its fleet, achieving at the outbreak of war a fleet with a low average age. That policy continued after the war: and had, indeed, during it, with the acquisition of no fewer than 43 buses under the Ministry of War Transport allocation scheme. With the exception of one Leyland, these were all Guy Arabs, built to an austere specification laid down by the Ministry of Supply, with bodywork generally to a similar utilitarian style. Production of wartime chassis under this scheme probably made Guy what it was as a passenger vehicle manufacturer in the postwar years; Midland General, no more than many other operators perforce obliged to accept such a novelty during the war, would not have bought Guys had AECs still been available.

Perhaps the "face" of Midland General, no less than of Mansfield District, was the AEC Regent carrying bodywork by Weymann's Motor Bodies, of Addlestone. Some of them were a little unusual in that they were diverted to London Transport as the first 20 members of the lowbridge RLH class; 35 Leyland PS1 Tigers, again bodied by Weymann, were diverted to Crosville. These transfers were the price paid for having modernised the fleet so thoroughly - the BTC considered that those 55 new vehicles could more usefully be employed elsewhere without detriment to Midland General.

In the great changes of the early 1970s, Midland General was merged with the Trent Motor Traction Company Ltd. Thus the "Midland General Group" passed away.

The Group's vehicle policy did not crystallize around the Weymann-bodied AEC until 1932. Before that Tilling-Stevens and Leylands had been purchased, and there had been a few Guys, Thornycrofts and Vulcans. AEC did not have it all its own way, however, as Midland General bought Leyland Tigers for single-deck work. Notts & Derby, after it ceased to operate trolleybuses, generally followed Midland General in its vehicle policy.

During the war, as we have seen, utility Guys were all that were available, and although the prewar policy was taken up again as soon as postwar conditions allowed, the inevitable switch to Eastern Coach Works-bodied Bristols, following nationalisation, began in 1954. After nationalisation and right up to the demise of the Group and its three separate companies, there was considerable movement of vehicles from one fleet to the other.

Acknowledgements

As so often with the writer's productions, others have contributed much, grateful thanks to all: the extensive written records of Ron Maybray have provided much invaluable detail; publication No. PE3 of The PSV Circle has proved most useful; Alan Oxley, John Senior and Bob Rowe have read the text and made a number of improvements; David and Mary Shaw have read the proofs; all photographs are from the John Banks Collection and were taken, unless otherwise stated, by Geoffrey Atkins. To readers wishing to know more about the history of the Midland General group, the book "Midland General" by Alan Oxley (Robin Hood Publishing, 1999) is strongly recommended.

John Banks,
Romiley, Cheshire
March 2003

Part One - Notts & Derby

Above: The first Notts & Derby trolleybuses were a batch of six English Electric single-deckers with forward-entrance bodywork, also by English Electric, seating 32. Numbers 300-5 (RB 5568-73) entered service in 1932; all were withdrawn in 1937 and sold to the Mexborough & Swinton system. This one is No. **302 (RB 5570)**, photographed at Nottingham Road, Ilkeston in May 1935.

Below: In 1932 there was also a batch of ten AEC 662T-English Electric trolleybuses, again with EE 32-seat bodywork, Nos 306-15 (RB 6613-22), of which No. **313 (RB 6620)** is seen in Milton Street, Nottingham, in December 1934. These vehicles were withdrawn between 1941 and 1948.

Above: Double-deck trolleybuses appeared the following year, 1933, as a batch of 15 AEC 661T-English Electric chassis, Nos 317-31 (RB 8951-65), fitted with 55-seat rear-entrance bodywork by the Metropolitan-Cammell Carriage & Wagon Company. Like the 1932 AEC-EEC single-deckers, these vehicles had an air intake in the form of a dummy radiator that - together with the half-cab layout - gave them much the same appearance as contemporary motor buses. The first of the batch, No. **317** (**RB 8951**), was photographed at Langley Mill in 1933.

Below: Number **319** (**RB 8953**) is seen at Gregory Boulevard, Nottingham, heading out on the long run to Ripley in February 1934. Although route numbers were shown in timetables from 1929, they were not displayed on vehicles until 1936, when prefixes were added.

Above: Although there was no reason why trolleybuses should not have had half-cabs and air intakes in the form of radiators (after all, electrical equipment needed cooling too), the norm for such vehicles became established before the war as a fully fronted design with flat panels below the windscreens. Seven Notts & Derby vehicles, Nos 300-5/32 (DRB 616-22), were thus turned out in 1937 by Weymann, of Addlestone, as 56-seat double-deckers on AEC 661T-EEC chassis. The first six took fleet numbers 300-5 vacated by the 1932 English Electrics. Number **302 (DRB 618)** is seen out in the country near Codnor, not far from its terminus at Ripley, in August 1940. Wartime white markings and one masked headlamp are evident.

Below: Five similar vehicles came in 1941, Nos 333-7 (HNU 826-30), of which No. **337 (HNU 830)** is seen at Church Street, Basford, in September 1946.

Above: In the darkest days of the war a further five AEC-EEC/Weymann trolleybuses, Nos 338-42 (HNU 970-4), were delivered. This 1942 batch is represented by No. **340 (HNU 972)**, seen in April 1953 at Gregory Boulevard, Nottingham, on a timing to Langley Mill.

Below: The entire fleet of Notts & Derby trolleybuses was sold, upon abandonment of the system, to Bradford Corporation. In this April 1953 view at the King Street/Queen Street terminus in Nottingham, No. **341 (HNU 973)** has, pending that move north, already been painted in Bradford livery though retaining for the time being the NDT crest.

Above: The last trolleybuses purchased for the Notts & Derby system came in 1949 and consisted of a batch of 15 BUT 9611T-EEC chassis, again with Weymann 56-seat bodies. BUT (British United Traction) was a joining of forces by AEC and Leyland for the production of trolleybus chassis. The batch was 343-57 (NNU 224-38): No. **344 (NNU 225)** was photographed in August 1950 turning into Mansfield Road, Nottingham, from Gregory Boulevard.

Below: In a photograph dating from the same month, No. **349 (NNU 230)** is in Milton Street, Nottingham, at Victoria railway station, on its way into the city. The blind for the return trip to Ripley has already been set by the driver.

Above: Nineteen-forty-nine BUT No. **354** (**NNU 235**) stands in the sun at the King Street/Queen Street terminus in Nottingham. The vehicle was very recently into service in this June 1949 view. The location is little more than 100 yards from Nottingham's Council House, where the photographer spent some of his career with Nottingham City Council.

Below: Number **347** (**NNU 228**), another of the 1949 BUTs, had the doleful duty of operating the last Notts & Derby trolleybus departure from Nottingham to Ripley on the night of 26th April 1953. The event was attracting little attention, quite unlike the scenes at 347's new home, Bradford, when that system was abandoned almost two decades later.

Motor buses rather took second place to trolleybuses in the Notts & Derby fleet until the 1953 abandonment: apart from one AEC Y type, those used before that date were owned and operated on hire to NDT by the associated Midland General concern. Five 1932 Tilling-Stevens D60A6 double-deckers with Weymann 50-seat rear-entrance bodywork were thus used to cover statutory services until overhead wiring was completed. The batch was Nos 121-5 (RB 6608-12) and our pictures are of Nos **124/5 (RB 6611/2)**. Both were working to Ripley circa 1935. All five were withdrawn in 1945. Midland General continued to provide buses for the B1 service and later the A4 Limited Stop between Ripley and Nottingham.

Above: In advance of its own batch of trolleybus-replacement Bristol KSW motor buses, Notts & Derby borrowed Brighton Hove & District No. **6439 (GPM 502)**, seen at Mount Street, Nottingham, in August 1952. The vehicle was in red and cream livery, but not to the Tilling standard, nor did it have the usual Tilling destination screen layout - both consequences of an agreement with Brighton Corporation.

Below: Notts & Derby's Eastern Coach Works-bodied 60-seat Bristol KSW6Gs came in 1953 as a batch of 15, Nos 300-14 (SRB 528-42), and one of them, No. **312 (SRB 540)**, is seen in May of that year at Mount Street. The next generation was already being planned: Crosville's Bristol Lodekka **RFM 406** was on trial on route B1 to Ripley. Midland General No. **168 (KRB 80)**, a 1947 Weymann-bodied AEC Regent II, is also visible.

Above: Brand new No. **311** (**SRB 539**) has just arrived at Langley Mill depot on 15th March 1953 from the Eastern Coach Works factory at Lowestoft. It still has ECW publicity in the windows. The batch was withdrawn in 1968/9.

Below: Another shot of one of the Bristol KSW6Gs in its first few weeks of service appears in another Mount Street picture, this time dating from August 1953 and depicting No. **309** (**SRB 537**) awaiting its departure time on the E1 to Strelley Lane.

The next new vehicles for the Notts & Derby fleet were delivered in 1957/8 and were on two varieties of the Bristol Lodekka chassis. The first (and the only delivery in 1957) was a solitary example of the rare LDL6G Lodekka variant - a 30ft-long rear-entrance 70-seater. Number **464 (13 DRB)** had platform doors fitted in 1964 and was withdrawn in 1971, later running for South Wales Transport. These views in August 1958 were taken on different occasions at Mount Street bus station, Nottingham. On the back of the nearside longitudinal seat can be seen the slogan "Travel by bus shipshape and *Bristol* fashion".

Above: In a direct comparison with the 30ft-long LDL6G Lodekka, here is an example of the 27ft 6ins standard LD6G 58-seat version, from which it will be seen that the bay between the rear axle and the platform is noticeably shorter. Number **472 (21 DRB)** was part of the 1958 batch of nine, Nos 465-73 (14-22 DRB), and was photographed in March 1958, again at Mount Street. The batch was withdrawn from service in 1970/1.

Below: Number **468 (17 DRB)** appears alongside No. **451 (970 ARA)**, a 1956 LD6G Lodekka in the Midland General fleet, in an April 1958 photograph taken to contrast the provision and absence of platform doors on this model.

Above: Later Lodekkas, delivered new in 1965 and 1968, were of the FLF forward-entrance, 70-seat version, with either Gardner (FLF6G) or Bristol (FLF6B) engines. **DNU 15C** of 1965, fleet number 635 when new, is seen in April 1973, after transfer to Midland General (renumbered as **706**). It is still in MGOC livery, but with light grey wheels, which contrasts with the standard poppy-red and white NBC livery seen on a Midland General FLF Lodekka alongside. **JNU 983D** had been MGOC No. 663 when new in 1966, but had been renumbered **720** by the time of this photograph. The location was Mount Street bus station, Nottingham.

Below: Six FLF6G Lodekkas - Nos 301-6 (TRB 568-73F) - delivered to Notts & Derby in 1968 are represented by No. **306** (**TRB 573F**) at Maid Marian Way, Nottingham, in November 1969.

Part Two - Midland General

Above: The first MGOC motorbuses were a pair of Vulcans in 1922. From 1923 to 1926 single-deck Guys, of type BA or BB, were specified. There were two BBs in 1924, fitted with Strachan & Brown dual-doorway 32-seat bodywork, numbered 5 and 6 with registrations NU 3564/5. Originally on solid tyres, they were later converted to run on pneumatics. Thus equipped, one of them is seen in Parliament Street, Nottingham, not long before its withdrawal in 1929. *(Photographer unknown)*

Below: In 1926 a trio of Leyland-bodied Leyland Z5 20-seaters was acquired from the Midland Motor Bus Company, of Kimberley. Numbered 17-9 by MGOC, they were registered NN 8868/9 and 9437. This one is No. **17 (NN 8868)**, parked in Wollaton Street, Nottingham, before the takeover. Numbers 17/8 were withdrawn later in 1926 and No. 19 in 1932. *(Photographer unknown)*

Above: Midland General began a substantial intake of Tilling-Stevens buses in 1927, starting in that year with no fewer than 22 - fleet numbers 25-46 with various registrations in the RA sequence - of either type B9B or B10B, all 31-seaters, with bodies by Davidson or Strachan & Brown. The picture is of No. **41** (**RA 3958**), one of the Strachan & Brown B10B models. It lasted in the fleet until 1931. *(Photographer unknown)*

Below: Number **38** (**RA 3872**), another of the Strachan & Brown-bodied B10Bs, was photographed in July 1929 at Skegness, having conveyed a private party to that bracing resort. This one was withdrawn in 1937 and found a new owner in Newport Pagnell.

Above: Nineteen-twenty-eight's intake of Tilling-Stevens chassis were forward-control models on the B10A chassis. A batch of six, Nos 56-61, were registered RA 6238/9/322-5, and we illustrate No. **59** (**RA 6323**), which had a Strachan & Brown 32-seat body. It was in Wollaton Street, Nottingham, in September 1929.

Below: Fifteen of the Tilling-Stevens B10A2 model came in 1931. RB 3844-58 had a somewhat mixed batch of fleet numbers: 27-9, 32/3, 40, 30/1, 35, 41, 38 and 42-5. Bodywork (five each) came from Ransomes, Strachan & Brown and Cowieson. The first of the batch, and one of five bodied by Ransomes, No. **27** (**RB 3844**), is seen at the north end of the Promenade in Skegness in June 1936. The bus was withdrawn in 1947.

Above: A crisp image, from the manufacturer's official photograph of a brand-new vehicle, of one of the Ransomes-bodied group of five. This is one of Nos 27-9, 32/3 (RB 3844-8).

Below: The Strachan-bodied quintet was RB 3849-52/4 - fleet numbers 40, 30/1/5/8 - of which No. **35 (RB 3852)** was photographed at Huntingdon Street, Nottingham, in March 1932 on layover before moving into the nearby bus station to take up its timing to Langley Mill. Some of these 1931 machines survived into 1947, but No. 35 went in 1945. As so often with time-served buses of that era, it found further work with a travelling fairground showman - a once rich source of fascinating former buses that criss-crossed the country in various stages of reconstruction and dilapidation.

Above: The last new Tilling-Stevens single-deckers for the Midland General group were of type B39A7 with 32-seat front-entrance bodies by John C Beadle, of Dartford, Kent. A batch of six was numbered 86-91 and had registrations RB 6013-8. Number **88 (RB 6015)** is seen at Huntingdon Street bus station, Nottingham, in November 1936. It was withdrawn in 1947.

Below: In 1931 the "SMA" fleet of J G Severn & Company (Severn's Motor Auctions Ltd), of Alfreton, was acquired. Eight vehicles, all with ADC or AEC chassis, were taken over, of which the earliest was **RA 6969**, a 1928 ADC 416 with Hall Lewis 32-seat bodywork. It was numbered 126 by MGOC but is illustrated before the transfer in an August 1930 photograph taken at Wollaton Street, Nottingham. It was withdrawn in 1937 and ended up with a fairground showman.

Above: Midland General No. **53** (**RA 8791**) was an ex-J G Severn ADC 416, again with Hall Lewis 32-seat bodywork. Hall, Lewis & Co was the predecessor of the Park Royal coachbuilding concern. New in 1929, this vehicle was withdrawn in 1937 and was later sold to a dealer in Sheffield.

Below: The only J G Severn double-decker, which became Midland General No. 108, was **JA 1291**, a former AEC demonstrator. The 1930 Short Brothers-bodied 50-seat Regent is shown working for Severn in April of that year. It was still owned by AEC and rather crude paper stickers in the windows and destination screen announced that it was running for SMA. The photograph was taken at Huntingdon Street bus station, Nottingham. Number 108 lasted in the MGOC fleet until 1946.

Above: The most modern ex-J G Severn vehicle was **RB 3864**, a 1931 AEC Regal with 32-seat front-entrance bodywork by Willowbrook, of Loughborough. It became Midland General No. **81** and was among the longest-lived ex-Severn buses, lasting until it and three similar Regals were withdrawn in 1949. In this October 1933 picture it was at Kent Street, Nottingham.

Below: Williamson's Garage Ltd, of Heanor, became an MGOC subsidiary in January 1928. The fleet continued in the associate company's ownership until January 1943, although vehicles were painted in Midland General livery from July 1931 when MGO took over the stage-carriage licences. Williamson's **NU 9050**, an Eaton-bodied Reo Pullman of 1926, was sold in May 1933. *(Photographer unknown)*

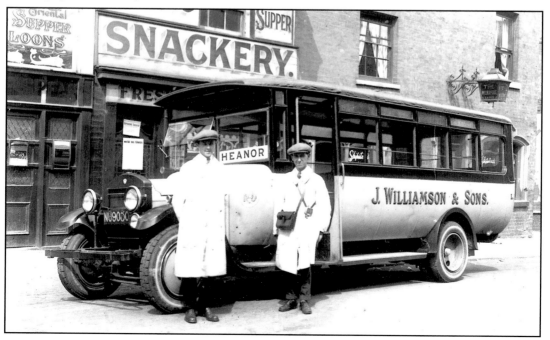

Above: Tansey & Severn Ltd, of Underwood, also became a Midland General associate company in 1931, and again was the owner of its fleet until 1943. During its period as an associate, T & S purchased a Leyland Titan TD1, two LT1 Lions and a pair of Tilling-Stevens. An earlier Lion, PLSC1 **RR 7716**, a 1927 Leyland-bodied 31-seater, is seen at Huntingdon Street in September 1934 in Midland General livery as No. **110**. It was withdrawn in 1937 and went on to serve a showman.

Below: This wonderful photograph, one of Geoffrey Atkins's most evocative, was taken one quiet Sunday morning in May 1933 at King Edward Street, Nottingham, and shows Tansey & Severn No. **104** (**RR 8605**), a 1928 PLSC3 35-seat Lion, again with Leyland bodywork. It was withdrawn in 1937.

Above: Tansey & Severn Leyland TD1 Titan **RR 9948** is seen in Midland General livery as No. **105**. Built in 1928, its Leyland body was a lowbridge 51-seater (27 upstairs and 24 down) with outside staircase, a feature visible in this August 1936 view at Huntingdon Street bus station. The vehicle was withdrawn in 1945, passed to Makemson, Bulwell, and subsequently to a showman.

Below: The TD1 purchased by Tansey & Severn during its associate status was No. **109** (**VO 3486**). This one dated from 1930 and was also a 51-seater, but its Leyland body had an enclosed staircase. It is seen in Parliament Street, Nottingham, with a Nottingham tram and a trolleybus in the background, in May 1933. This one survived into 1947 and also saw further service with a fairground showman.

Above: In a scene depicting the exodus to resorts such as Skegness from Nottingham Huntingdon Street on a sunny Saturday morning in the early 1930s, Tansey & Severn No. **109 (VO 3486)** appears again, in a rare rear view. Some of the holidaymakers are to be treated to a long and perhaps breezy journey in the Trent Motor Traction Company's No. **604 (CH 6260)**, a 1927 SOS QC all-weather coach, waiting with its roof already folded down in the summer sunshine. Luggage is being loaded into a Trent van, whose open door is just visible on the left of the picture. In the background is a very rare - for that date - Mercedes-Benz motor lorry. If ever a picture limned and hymned a vanished age, this is it.

Below: The Tansey & Severn Leyland LT1 Lions purchased in 1929 after Midland General took an interest in the company were VO 1827/8, given fleet numbers 115 and 64. This is No. **115 (VO 1827)** at Huntingdon Street in February 1935. Its Leyland body had 35 seats.

Above: Second-hand Leylands entered the fleet when the business of F Porter & Sons, of Stonebroom, was taken over in 1933. Of four Leyland LT Lions (three LT1 and one LT2) from the Porter fleet, we illustrate **RA 9628**, a 1929 LT1 with 32-seat Davidson bodywork. As Midland General No. **85**, it is seen in Huntingdon Street, Nottingham, in March 1934. After withdrawal in 1939 it was converted as a lorry. Davidson, of Trafford Park, was the precursor of the Reeve & Kenning concern.

Below: The Alfreton Motor Transport Company Ltd was another that became an associate company of Midland General, this time in 1936, and remained so until 1943. Some years before the merger, **RA 5970**, a 1928 Leyland-bodied Lion PLSC3 35-seater, was at Skegness Lawn motor park in July 1929. As an associate vehicle, it would become No. 150 in 1936 and last only until 1938. After withdrawal it became - almost inevitably, it seems - fairground transport.

Above: Although Weymann bodywork had been specified on the 1932 Tilling-Stevens double-deckers *(see page 15)* and on AEC chassis from the same year for the Mansfield District fleet, the first Weymann-bodied AECs for Midland General did not arrive until 1936 in the shape of ten 32-seat front-entrance coaches, Nos 156-65 (CRA 655-64). Two of them, Nos **163** and **156** (**CRA 662** and **655**) are seen in a picture for which there are no details but which was probably at Skegness in an early postwar summer.

Below: Number **163** again, in the postwar period after a rebuild involving the fitting of a 7.7-litre AEC diesel engine, the loss of its roof-mounted luggage rack and changes to trim and livery. The picture was taken at Broad Marsh, Nottingham, in April 1956.

Above: The AEC/Weymann combination was to become the early postwar "face" of the Midland General group fleets until superseded by the Eastern Coach Works Bristol following nationalisation. A batch of 25 double-deckers for Midland General in 1937 had 52-seat front-entrance bodies from the Addlestone coachbuilder, epitomised by No. **16** (**DNU 960**), seen at Mount Street, Nottingham, in September 1939.

Below: The photograph above was taken in the month during which war was declared on Germany. One of the results of that is seen in this August 1940 picture of the same bus near Wollaton heading for Ilkeston and fitted with headlamp masks and white markings for blackout use.

Above: Weymann coachwork also featured on substantial numbers of Leyland Tiger TS7 and TS8 chassis in the late 1930s. From a 1937 batch of ten TS7s with dual-purpose 35-seat front-entrance coachwork we show No. **83 (DRA 163)** in an August 1953 scene at Matlock bus station. By then the bodywork had been substantially rebuilt. Number 83 was withdrawn in 1955.

Below: The 1938 batch of five Weymann-bodied Leyland Tigers were on the TS8 chassis. Number **144 (ERA 920)**, the last of the batch, was also at Matlock bus station, this time in August 1955, a year before its withdrawal from service and sale to a Salford dealer. A postwar Leyland PS1/1 with Saunders bodywork from the Midland General fleet stands in the background.

Above: In 1938 Weymann dual-purpose bodies on AEC Regal chassis came in 35- and 32-seat versions. One of the latter was No. **171 (ERA 925)**, one of a batch of seven. It was photographed in Granby Street, Nottingham, in May 1948. This Regal was withdrawn from service as late as 1959, and even at that age it found further use as a staff bus in Spalding, Lincolnshire.

Below: Ten AEC Regents - Nos 174-83 (FNU 169-78) - arrived after the Regals and Tigers in 1938. The Weymann bodies were generally similar to those on the 1937 machines. Number **176 (FNU 171)** was also in Granby Street, Nottingham, just over three years later in August 1951. The bus was withdrawn in 1955 and sold to the Leeds dealer W North.

<< Opposite page: Granby Street, Nottingham, is again the location for this June 1950 view featuring fore and aft angles of Weymann-bodied AEC Regents. Number **178** (**FNU 173**) of 1938 and No. **58** (**DNU 971**) of 1937 are the stars, abetted by a utility Guy Arab No. **11** (**HRB 981**) carrying a Northern Counties body.

Above: Fifteen Leyland Tiger TS8s with Weymann dual-purpose bodywork of 32- or 35-seat capacity were delivered in 1939. Number **135** (**FRB 85**), a 35-seater, was the first of them, and it is seen at Ilkeston garage in August 1949.

Below: Number **153** (**FRB 717**) at Broad Marsh, Nottingham, in September 1955, had had its 35-seat body rebuilt, considerably altering its appearance.

Above: Llanelly & District, another Balfour Beatty company, was the source of two similar 35-seat vehicles transferred to Midland General in 1938. They were Nos 184/5 (ABX 78/9), of which No. **184 (ABX 78)** is seen at Mount Street, Nottingham, in April 1952.

Below: At the outbreak of war all bus manufacture was frozen by government decree. Vehicles that could be constructed from parts already available were later authorised, and became known as "unfrozen". One such vehicle came to Midland General in 1942: No. **186 (HRA 417)** was a Leyland-bodied highbridge 56-seat Titan TD7, originally intended for Western SMT. In this view, another at Mount Street, in July 1949 it retains its distinctive Scottish destination screen arrangement.

Above: The unfrozen Leyland Titan TD7 had, by the time of this December 1956 picture, also taken at Mount Street, had its destination screen arrangement rebuilt to Midland General standard. For such a non-standard vehicle it lasted remarkably well, and was withdrawn in 1959 and scrapped the following year.

Below: When renewed bus production was officially sanctioned, Guy Motors was the principal chassis manufacturer. Midland General took many Guy Arabs up to 1946 but started quietly with just two, one each bodied by Brush and Weymann, Gardner 5LW-engined Mark I Arabs in 1942. Number **187 (HRA 682)** was the very first, though our illustration shows it in October 1954 after the Brush body had been rebuilt (by Bond) with rubber-mounted windows. Another Mount Street picture.

Above: All sorts of odd things happened during the early part of the war involving the unfrozen chassis and bodies and the utility, or austerity, chassis as the government approved and controlled production came to be known. Number **188 (HRA 815)**, seen in March 1952, was the second Guy Arab I in 1942, and its Weymann-finished Metro-Cammell body had been intended for Manchester Corporation.

Below: There was also a pair of Gardner 5LW-engined Guy Arab Is in 1943, one of which also had a Weymann/MCCW Manchester body. The second, No. **190 (HRB 17)**, had a body, also by Weymann, that should have gone to Liverpool Corporation. In this May 1953 - Coronation Year - view at Stockwell Gate, Mansfield, it carries a device reading "God Save the Queen" at the bottom of its radiator. Number 190 was withdrawn in 1960 and sold to the operator Camm, of Nottingham.

Above: Weymann also built utility (or austerity) bodies to the specification of the Ministry of War Transport to a design, like those of other coachbuilders engaged in similar work, that sternly did away with any pretence at luxury, and banned all unnecessary curves in the domes and profiles. Midland General had six of these in 1943, represented in original condition by No. **193** (**HRB 424**), seen at Mount Street in May 1949.

Below: Northern Counties, of Wigan, produced many utility bodies on wartime Guy Arab chassis, including a number for Midland General, of which eleven were delivered in 1944. One of them was No. **22** (**HRB 982**), again photographed in substantially original condition at Mount Street, this time in April 1953.

Above: All the utility bodies discussed so far were of the highbridge layout; in 1945/6 there were lowbridge examples from Roe, Weymann and Strachan. Number **208** (**JNU 683**) was a Roe example, a 55-seater delivered in 1945 as the fourth of a batch of six (Nos 205-10) whose delivery spilled over into 1946. It is shown at Huntingdon Street bus station, Nottingham, in August 1946.

Below: There were also five lowbridge 55-seaters from Weymann in 1945, three of which were rebuilt by Bond, of Wythenshawe, Manchester, in 1953: they thus lasted into 1959, only two years longer than the two unrebuilt examples. Rebuilt No. **403** - originally 203 - (**JNU 678**) was photographed at Beetwell Street, Chesterfield, in June 1956.

Above: Nineteen-forty-four Guy No. **7** (**HRB 979**), a 56-seater bodied by Northern Counties, was one of a number of highbridge utilities to be rebuilt in the mid 1950s, in this case again by Bond who handled most such work, although Midland General rebuilt two of the 1944 buses. In this rare rear view, No. 7 is at Mount Street alongside No. **59** (**DNU 972**), one of the 1937 forward-entrance Weymann-bodied AEC Regents.

Below: More substantial remedial work on the six 1945/6 Roe-bodied lowbridge machines Nos 405-10 (originally 205-10) involved converting them to highbridge 58-seaters with new Eastern Coach Works bodies. The work was done in 1955 and caused a further renumbering, to 102-7. Number **105** (**JNU 683**) was at Stockwell Gate, Mansfield, in March 1956. The last of these rebodied buses was withdrawn in 1968.

Above: The Company was not slow to return to AEC for chassis once the war was over and in 1946 both Regals and Regents were obtained. The Regals were four - Nos 41-4 (JRB 127-30) - fitted with Duple 35-seat dual-purpose bodies. The first of them, No. **41** (**JRB 127**), was at Mount Street in March 1950. It was withdrawn in 1960 and went on to work for Nottingham Education Committee.

Below: There were also eight AEC Regent II chassis in 1946 and for these the Company was able to obtain Weymann bodies, thus restoring its prewar standard, although in the light of experience with problems they were to rear- rather than forward-entrance specification. Again we illustrate the first of a batch, in the shape of No. **60** (**KNU 601**), in a February 1951 view at Mount Street. Number 60 was withdrawn and sold to a dealer in 1962.

Above: Duple 35-seat dual-purpose bodies similar to those on the four 1946 AEC Regals appeared on a pair of Leyland PS1/1 Tigers in 1947. Their fleet and registration numbers followed on from the Regals as 45/6 (JRB 131/2). Number **45 (JRB 131)** was photographed at Broad Marsh, Nottingham, in December 1953. It was withdrawn in 1959.

Below: Six Bedford OBs with Duple 29-seat coachwork also appeared in 1947. KRB 65-70 had, as so often with Midland General, haphazard fleet numbers: in this case 103/5/14/34/41/8; all six were withdrawn in 1952 and five of them were exported. The picture, at Skegness in July 1949, is of No. **103 (KRB 65)**, which went on export to Associated Motorways, Colombo, Ceylon.

Above: A batch of 25 Leyland Tiger PS1/1 chassis in 1948 were bodied by Saunders, of Beaumaris, Anglesey. All were dual-purpose, some with 32 seats and some with 35. Their original condition and livery is shown on the vehicle in the background, which was No. **223** (**KRB 109**). Number **221** (**KRB 107**) illustrates a substantial remodelling of beading and livery. An April 1952 view at Canal Street, Nottingham.

Below: The AEC Regent III with Weymann 56-seat rear-entrance bodywork became the new postwar standard. The first 15 were delivered in 1948 and in this July 1949 view at Mount Street the batch is represented by No. **89** (**MRB 34**), a bus that was withdrawn as an 18-year-old in 1966 and transferred for a short spell of further service in the Mansfield District fleet.

Above: Ten 53-seat lowbridge versions of the AEC Regent III/Weymann combination were delivered in 1950: a type familiar to London Transport enthusiasts as the RLH class - the nearest the Capital ever came to a lowbridge RT. Brand new No. **424** (**ONU 633**) was at Granby Street, Nottingham, in June 1950. It was withdrawn in 1968.

Below: In a November 1950 view at Mount Street, the unfrozen 1942 Leyland Titan TD7 No. **186** (**HRA 417**) shares the parking area with two of the 1950 lowbridge AEC Regent IIIs, Nos **423/5** (**ONU 632/4**).

Above: There were to be no more new buses until 1954, and by 1953 a shortage of vehicles was being felt at Midland General; in that year three 1939/40 Bristol K5Gs with Eastern Coach Works lowbridge 53-seat bodies were acquired from Hants & Dorset. These were about as far removed from an AEC Regent III with preselector gearbox and six-cylinder engine as was possible, but Midland General was now established as a Tilling operator and had to follow policy. **ERU 587** (fleet number **431**), formerly Hants & Dorset 1036, was at Matlock in May 1955, shortly before it and the other two were withdrawn, no doubt to sighs of relief from drivers.

Below: Although Notts & Derby had taken Bristol KSWs as trolleybus replacements in 1953, Midland General's first new Bristol double-deckers, in 1954, were LD6G Lodekkas, exemplified by No. **435** (**VRB 521**) at Derby bus station in December 1954.

Above: The Lodekkas were preceded in 1954 by a batch of six Bristol LS6G coaches with 39-seat bodies by Eastern Coach Works. Their arrival eased the load still being borne by the Leyland PS1/1 Tigers on coaching work. Number **230** (**URB 561**) was at the Lawn motor park, Skegness, in August 1955. It was withdrawn in 1966 and sold to Granville, Grimsby in March 1967.

Below: In 1955 the Bristol LS6G appeared in the form of dual-purpose 43-seaters, the Eastern Coach Works body being that normally used for stage-carriage vehicles rather than coaches. The first of a batch of ten, No. **232** (**XNU 413**) is shown on private hire work at Langworth, Lincolnshire, in August 1955. Withdrawn in 1969, it went on to join the Eastern Counties fleet.

Above: Bristol LD6G Lodekkas were added to the fleet in 1956 and 1957, a batch of five in the latter year being represented by No. **462** (**11 DRB**) at Mount Street in July 1959. The original production Lodekka radiator grille, as shown on page 48, soon gave way to a shorter version, as carried by No. 462. The entire batch of five was withdrawn in 1970 and sold to West Riding.

Below: The recently introduced Bristol MW, again to a 43-seat dual-purpose specification within the standard ECW service-bus shell, entered the Midland General fleet in 1958 as a batch of ten, Nos 254-63 (23-32 DRB). As with the other Bristol/ECW types in the fleet, the Midland General livery gave them a more attractive appearance than that of the average Tilling vehicle. Number **257** (**26 DRB**) was at Mount Street in 1958. It was transferred to United Counties in 1971.

Above: By 1961 the Lodekka was available in the revised F series, the FSF signifying a short chassis with forward-entrance bodywork. Midland General took a batch of ten across 1961/2, of which an example is No. **502** (**442 SNU**), an FSF6G (and therefore Gardner-engined) seen at Huntingdon Street bus station, Nottingham, in April 1966. The Eastern Coach Works body had 60 seats.

Below: By contrast, the FLF Lodekka was longer, at 30ft, and was usually a 70-seater. Midland General took both FLF6B and FLF6G versions, engined respectively by Bristol and Gardner. Number **660** (**JNU 980D**) was an FLF6G, delivered in 1966, which was photographed in March of that year when brand new. It was at Mount Street bus station, Nottingham.

Above: Bristol/ECW coaches on both the underfloor-engined MW6G chassis and the new rear-engined RE were purchased in the early 1960s. Number **128** - originally 282 - (**1379 R**) was a 1963 MW6G 39-seater with front entrance. In this May 1973 view at Nottingham Victoria, the plain front dome had been rebuilt to incorporate route number and destination screens.

Below: Three Bristol RELH6G coaches with 51-seat Eastern Coach Works bodies were delivered in 1964. Yet again, the Midland General blue and cream livery made a fine effect, in this case on coachwork that was already very striking. Although soon to be floating passengers to London in supreme comfort, in this view No. **32 (1386 R)** was providing luxurious stage-carriage transport on the Nottingham to Hucknall service. The November 1964 picture was taken at Broad Marsh bus station, Nottingham.

Above: The coach fleet was augmented in the late 1960s by a number of Bedfords fitted with Duple 41-seat coachwork. The first were a batch of three in 1967 - Nos 219-21 (ONU 919-21E) - of which we illustrate No. **219 (ONU 919E)** at Mount Street, Nottingham in September 1967.

Below: The rear-engined double-decker had been a power in the land since the late 1950s, though early models, especially of the Leyland Atlantean, had proved less than perfectly reliable. Bristol was late into this field: its rear-engined offering arrived in the shape of the VR in the late 1960s. Midland General took six in 1969, with ECW 70-seat bodies: the second numerically was No. **316 (BNU 680G)**, seen here at Maid Marian Way, Nottingham, in June 1969.

Above: The Bristol RE, which we have seen as the high-floorline RELH model, also came with a low floor as the RELL for stage-carriage work, in single- or dual-door versions. Midland General bought five 44-seat dual-door RELL6Gs in 1969 and they had the flat screen associated with earlier examples of the breed, exemplified by No. **136** (**DRB 303H**) at Huntingdon Street, Nottingham, in August 1969.

Below: Following the amalgamation within the National Bus Company of the former BET and Tilling operators, the former's curved windscreen design was applied to the latter's Bristol RE maximum-length service bus, as shown on No. **144** (**FRB 206H**), another 44-seat dual-door Bristol RELL6G, delivered into the Mansfield District fleet in 1970.

Part Three - Mansfield District

With the last picture on the previous page we have moved from Midland General to the Mansfield District Traction Company at the beginning of the 1970s, when the group as it had existed for some decades was on the threshold of much change; it is now time to go back and look at some of the earlier vehicles found in the green Mansfield District fleet, starting with No. **12 (RR 6948)**, a 1927 Leyland PLC1 Lioness, with Leyland 26-seat bodywork. This was one of six, registered RR 6600-2/948-50, which were later given the fleet numbers 9-14. This Lioness was withdrawn in 1937, passing to a Tredegar operator. Two of the six were still in Mansfield District service in 1945.

Above: A great rarity in British bus fleets was the Sunbeam chassis: uncommon among the few that were operated was the six-wheeled double-decker, the Sikh. This 1929 example, registered **UK 7456**, with 67-seat bodywork by Christopher Dodson, of Willesden, was originally a Sunbeam demonstrator and it was purchased by Mansfield District in 1931. By mid 1933 it had been sold to Derby Corporation and was scrapped in 1940. *(Photographer unknown)*

Below: Although the first four of the first batch of Mansfield District AEC Regents had bodywork by Short Brothers, of Rochester, bodies for the rest of the 34-strong batch - Nos 51-84, VO 8551-84 - were supplied by Weymann, to 54-seat rear-entrance specification. Number **58** (**VO 8558**) features in a May 1935 photograph at Westgate, Mansfield.

Above: The nearside view of the classic AEC Regent/Weymann combination is illustrated by No. **59** (**VO 8559**), photographed as passengers were alighting at Mansfield LMS railway station in September 1933. Numbers 58/9 illustrated here and on the previous page (also 57 and 60) were withdrawn in 1945 and later ran for Southend Corporation from 1946 to 1950.

Below: The AEC/Weymann vehicle in single-deck form came in 1933 when six Regal 4s with 32-seat bodies were delivered. The batch 85-90 (AAL 106-111) is represented by the last of them, No. **90** (**AAL 111**), at Huntingdon Street, Nottingham, in April 1935. Number 90 had a metal-framed body, unlike the other five. It was withdrawn in 1946.

Above: To answer a need for small buses, two Dennis Ace chassis were purchased in 1937. Numbers 49/50 (CRR 752/3) had front-entrance 20-seat bodies by John C Beadle, of Dartford. They lasted in the Mansfield District fleet until 1950 and No. **50** (**CRR 753**) was photographed in Queen Street, Mansfield, in September 1947.

Below: Also in 1937, two second-hand Leyland PLSC3 Lions with LMS Derby Works bodies were acquired from the London, Midland & Scottish Railway: CH 7901/6 were given fleet numbers 19/20. **CH 7901** is seen at Mansfield LMS railway station in May 1930, some time before passing to Mansfield District.

Above: AEC and Weymann continued to supply the by now familiar vehicles to Mansfield District and among 1937's deliveries was AEC Regent No. **97** (**DRR 671**), a 56-seat rear-entrance machine seen here in a postwar photograph at Stockwell Gate, Mansfield. Behind was the Trent Motor Traction Company's contemporary AEC Regent No. **1342** (**RC 4625**), originally also Weymann-bodied, but rebodied by Willowbrook in 1949.

Below: AEC Regent/Weymann No. **105** (**FNN 749**) of 1939 was a forward-entrance 52-seater, seen here in wartime condition in a picture taken in Newark.

Above: Mansfield District took delivery of utility Guy Arabs in 1944/5: eight highbridge with Strachan or Northern Counties bodies and two lowbridge Weymann examples. One of the latter, **GRR 62**, is seen after transfer to Midland General as No. **215** in 1946. The picture was taken in Stockwell Gate, Mansfield, in May 1953. It was heading for Clay Cross, a location well known to many tramcar enthusiasts.

Below: Number **112** (**GNN 300**) was one of six Northern Counties-bodied highbridge Guy Arabs dating from 1944. All had their bodies rebuilt by Bond in 1953, with the attractive results shown in this March 1954 view at Westgate, Mansfield.

Above: Mansfield District made a good start on its postwar fleet replacement in 1946/7 with no fewer than 40 AEC Regent IIs with Weymann 56-seat rear-entrance bodies. By 1948 the model had advanced to the Regent III and a further 22 were purchased, with similar bodywork. The 1948 Regent IIIs are exemplified by No. **143** (**JVO 939**) seen in Mansfield in April 1956.

Below: In 1950, the 23-strong AEC and Daimler fleet of the Ebor Bus Company Ltd, of Mansfield, was acquired by Mansfield District. One of the AECs was No. **118** (**HAL 841**), a Regent II with Eastern Coach Works 56-seat bodywork. This unusual combination was photographed in Mansfield with a lowbridge utility Daimler, also ex-Ebor, behind.

Above: New single-deckers arrived in 1949 when 24 AEC Regal IIIs were delivered. Bodywork, to dual-purpose 35-seat specification, was by Weymann. The batch was Nos 5-28 (KRR 251-74) and we illustrate No. **20** (**KRR 266**) in original condition and livery at the Lawn motor park, Skegness, in June 1949. Despite the "dual-purpose" classification, the seats seem to be to ordinary service-bus specification with low backs and metal grab-handles.

Below: The same vehicle is seen at Nottingham's Broad Marsh bus station in July 1955 with revised beading and livery, and higher-backed seats more appropriate to the coaching and private hire duties on which these vehicles were frequently used.

Above: The fleet of Bevan and Barker Ltd, of Mansfield, acquired by Mansfield District in 1957, was rather conveniently all AEC, though there were no Weymann bodies. Number **164 (LRR 207)** was a 1950 AEC Regent III bodied as a 56-seater by Crossley, of Stockport. It ran for Mansfield District until 1968.

Below: As with the other members of the Midland General group, Mansfield District was eventually to buy Bristol/ECW products. LS6G coaches and LD6G Lodekkas had been taken into stock in 1954 and 1955 saw more Lodekkas and some LS6G dual-purpose 43-seaters, an example of which was brand new No. **208 (SNN 70)**, seen here in Westgate, Mansfield, in May 1955.

Above: The prospect of replacing the Weymann/Regent with the ECW/Lodekka was a real one given the group's nationalised status. Here, at Mansfield Woodhouse in March 1951, is a harbinger of what was to come, as West Yorkshire's No. **822** (**JWT 712**) was being appraised by Mansfield District. Whatever its technical merits (or demerits in the case of this divided-transmission prototype), few would disagree that the 1948 AEC Regent/Weymann, No. **150** (**JVO 946**), alongside was much the more attractive visually.

Below: The production Lodekkas were much neater and tidier, as seen on brand new No. **505** (**SNN 73**), new in 1955 and photographed at Huntingdon Street in September of that year.